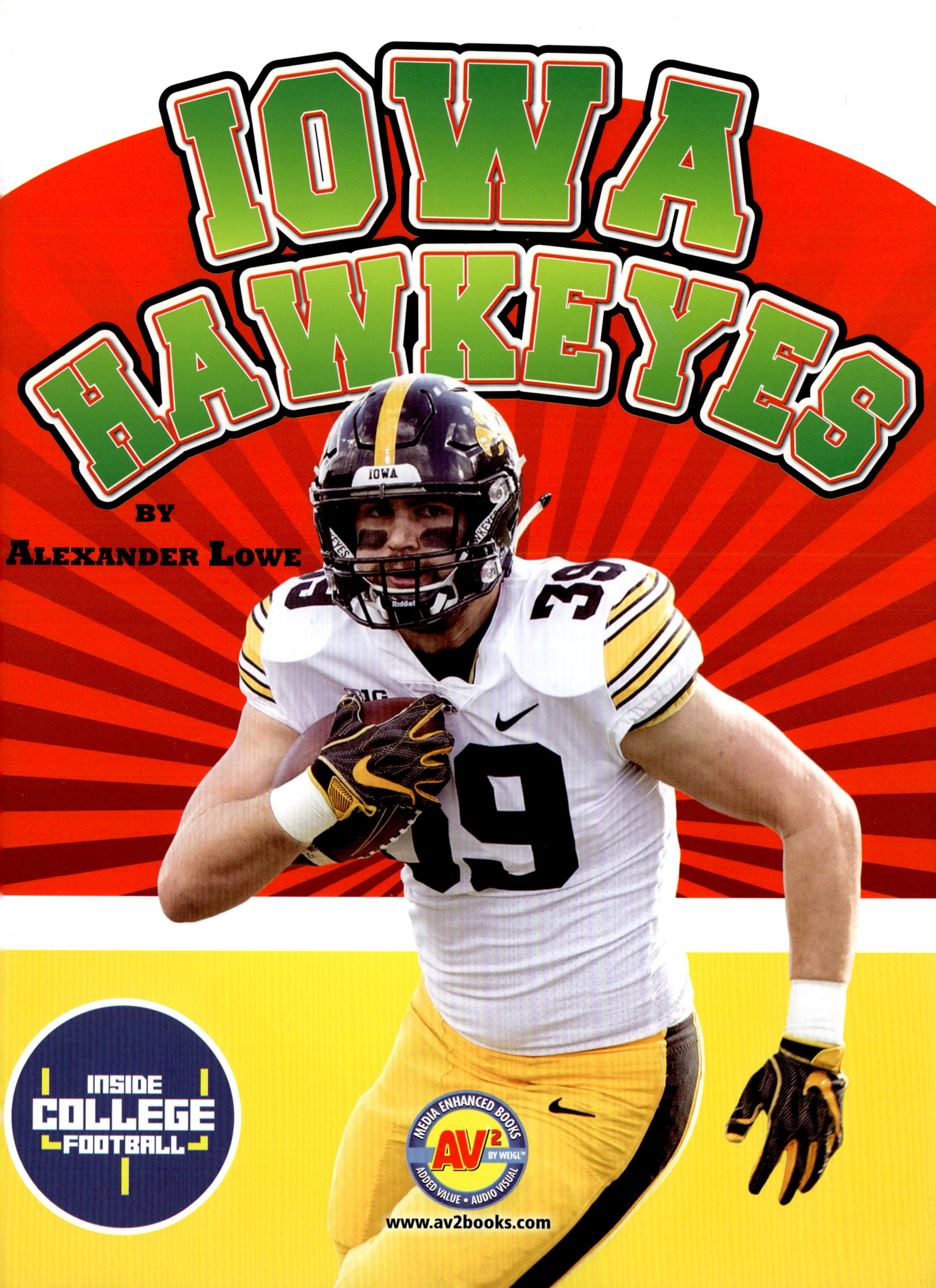
IOWA HAWKEYES
BY
ALEXANDER LOWE
INSIDE COLLEGE FOOTBALL
MEDIA ENHANCED BOOKS
AV2 BY WEIGL
ADDED VALUE • AUDIO VISUAL
www.av2books.com

Go to www.av2books.com, and enter this book's unique code.

BOOK CODE

AVD64298

AV² by Weigl brings you media enhanced books that support active learning.

AV² provides enriched content that supplements and complements this book. Weigl's AV² books strive to create inspired learning and engage young minds in a total learning experience.

Your AV² Media Enhanced books come alive with...

Audio
Listen to sections of the book read aloud.

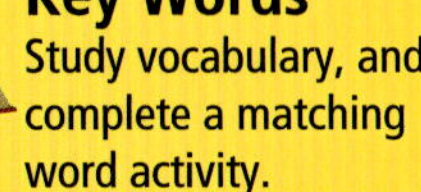

Key Words
Study vocabulary, and complete a matching word activity.

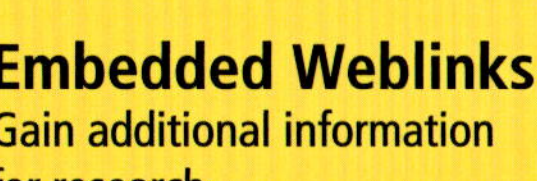

Video
Watch informative video clips.

Quizzes
Test your knowledge.

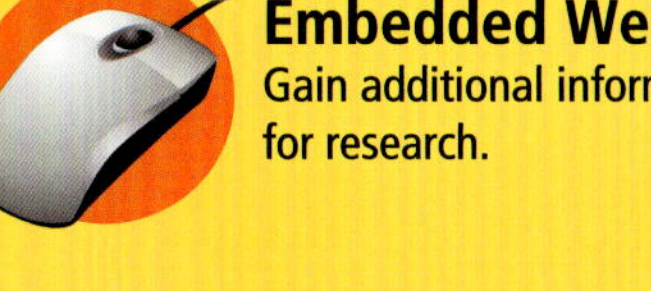

Embedded Weblinks
Gain additional information for research.

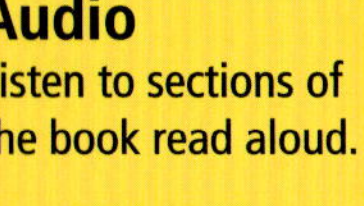

Slideshow
View images and captions, and prepare a presentation.

Try This!
Complete activities and hands-on experiments.

... and much, much more!

Published by AV² by Weigl
350 5th Avenue, 59th Floor
New York, NY 10118
Website: www.av2books.com

Library of Congress Control Number: 2018968222

ISBN 978-1-7911-0126-8 (hardcover)
ISBN 978-1-7911-0127-5 (multi-user eBook)
ISBN 978-1-7911-0128-2 (single-user eBook)

Printed in Guangzhou, China
1 2 3 4 5 6 7 8 9 0 23 22 21 20 19

042019
102318

Project Coordinator: Jared Siemens   Designer: Terry Paulhus

Every reasonable effort has been made to trace ownership and to obtain permission to reprint copyright material. The publishers would be pleased to have any errors or omissions brought to their attention so that they may be corrected in subsequent printings.

The publisher acknowledges Alamy, Getty Images, and Wikimedia Commons as its primary image suppliers for this title.

Iowa Hawkeyes

CONTENTS

Introduction

For fans of the University of Iowa Hawkeyes, watching their team compete its way to the top of the Big Ten Conference is a treat every Saturday. Especially in the last 40 years, the team has been a national force. In that time, the Hawkeyes have won more than 490 games, including 16 bowl games.

It is not just on the field that the team excites its fans. Kinnick Stadium, home of the Hawkeyes, sits within view of the University of Iowa Stead Family Children's Hospital. At the end of the first quarter of every game, Iowa fans, players, and the marching band turn and wave at the kids looking down from the top floors.

Running back Ivory Kelly-Martin was one of only 10 Iowa true freshmen to play in the 2017 season, and is the first true freshman to rush for two touchdowns in a single game since 2010.

The Hawkeyes are also known for the way they enter the field. "The Swarm" is where all the players jog onto the field hand-in-hand. This show of **unity** sets the tone for how they play the game. Despite the state of Iowa not having any major professional sports teams, fans have plenty to cheer for during football season.

Ihmir Smith-Marsette played in 11 games and logged 18 catches for 187 yards with 2 touchdowns during the 2017 season, his first year of play for the Hawkeyes.

IOWA

Stadium Kinnick Stadium

Division Big Ten West

Head Coach Kirk Ferentz

Location Iowa City, Iowa

National Championships 0

Nicknames Hawkeyes

2
Retired Numbers

1
Heisman Memorial Trophy Winner

20
First-Round NFL Draft Picks

16
Bowl Game Victories

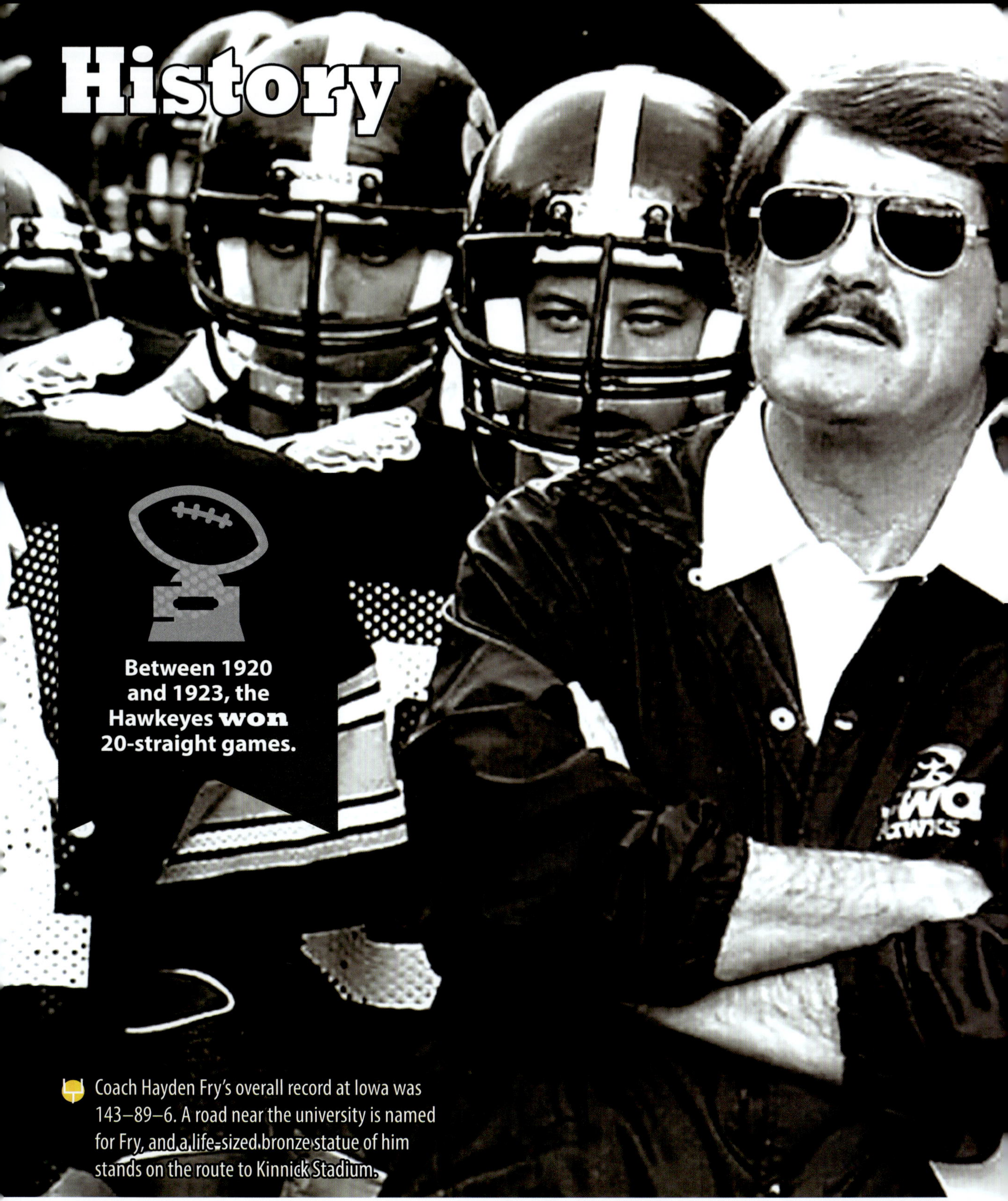

History

Between 1920 and 1923, the Hawkeyes **won** 20-straight games.

Coach Hayden Fry's overall record at Iowa was 143–89–6. A road near the university is named for Fry, and a life-sized bronze statue of him stands on the route to Kinnick Stadium.

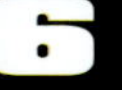

The first Iowa football team played in 1889. Ten years later, the team had its first undefeated season. After that, the Hawkeyes were invited to join the Western Conference, which was later renamed the Big Ten Conference. The Hawkeyes still play in the Big Ten today. In the 1920s, Coach Howard Jones took over and led the team to back-to-back Big Ten titles. In 1939, the team exceeded expectations, largely due to its best player, halfback Nile Kinnick. Kinnick won the 1939 **Heisman Memorial Trophy**. The team's stadium is named after him.

One of the most notable eras in Iowa history began in the late 1970s when Hayden Fry was hired to coach the team. He led the Hawkeyes for 20 years and took the team to 14 bowl games. The Hawkeyes also won three Big Ten titles during those 20 years.

The current era of Hawkeyes football has been just as successful. The team has played in 16 bowl games in the last 18 seasons. It has ended the season as high as number seven in the national rankings. Coach Kirk Ferentz has helped sustain the success that Iowa fans have come to expect.

Kinnick Stadium is the only college football venue in the country that is named for a Heisman Trophy winner. A large statue of Nile Kinnick stands outside the stadium's entrance.

The Stadium

Before every home game, Herky the Hawk leads the football team onto the field while AC/DC's "Back in Black" plays on the stadium's sound system.

The Hawkeyes play in Kinnick Stadium on the campus of the University of Iowa. The stadium first opened in October 1929. The initial construction was completed in only seven months. Crews worked around the clock to finish in time for the 1929 season.

There have been a few changes to the home of the Hawkeyes over the years. Originally known as Iowa Stadium, it was renamed in 1972 to honor the team's first Heisman winner, Nile Kinnick. More than 17,000 seats were added through four **renovations**. In 2004, a new press box and scoreboard were added.

There are a few things that make Kinnick Stadium stand out from other football fields. Coach Hayden Fry had the visitor's locker room painted pink in an effort to put opponents in a calmer mood. Now, the bright pink color is something many other teams dread. The stadium is also next door to the Iowa Children's Hospital. The hospital's Press Box Café is on the top floor and features an **unobstructed** view of the players, fans, and field, as well as a large-screen television where patients and their families can watch Iowa's away games.

The Kinnick Wave—when everyone in Kinnick Stadium turns and waves toward the University of Iowa Stead Family Children's Hospital—is a favorite tradition at the University of Iowa.

Where They Play

Welcome to Kinnick Stadium, home of the University of Iowa Hawkeyes. More than 69,000 fans fill the seats with black and gold. Players touch a statue of the stadium's namesake, Nile Kinnick, before they take the field. A winning spirit and time-honored traditions make Kinnick Stadium a great place for football.

BIG TEN WEST

1 **Northwestern University**
Evanston, Illinois

2 **Purdue University**
West Lafayette, Indiana

3 **University of Illinois**
Urbana-Champaign, Illinois

★ 4 **University of Iowa**
Iowa City, Iowa

5 **University of Minnesota**
Minneapolis, Minnesota

6 **University of Nebraska**
Lincoln, Nebraska

7 **University of Wisconsin**
Madison, Wisconsin

Arena
Kinnick Stadium

Location
Iowa City, Iowa

Broke Ground
March 1929

Completed
October 1929

Surface
Artificial Turf

Features
- 69,250-seat capacity
- 20-foot (6-meter) statue of Heisman Trophy winner Nile Kinnick
- If put in a line, the stadium's bleachers would stretch 20 miles (32 kilometers)

BIG TEN EAST

1 **Indiana University**
Bloomington, Indiana

2 **Michigan State University**
East Lansing, Michigan

3 **Ohio State University**
Columbus, Ohio

4 **Pennsylvania State University**
State College, Pennsylvania

5 **Rutgers University–New Brunswick**
New Brunswick–Piscataway, New Jersey

6 **University of Maryland**
College Park, Maryland

7 **University of Michigan**
Ann Arbor, Michigan

NORTH DAKOTA
MINNESOTA
WISCONSIN
MICHIGAN
NEW YORK
RHODE ISLAND
CONNECTICUT
SOUTH DAKOTA
PENNSYLVANIA
NEW JERSEY
IOWA
NEBRASKA
OHIO
DELAWARE
MARYLAND
ILLINOIS
INDIANA
WEST VIRGINIA
VIRGINIA
WASHINGTON, D.C.
KANSAS
MISSOURI
KENTUCKY
NORTH CAROLINA
TENNESSEE
SOUTH CAROLINA
OKLAHOMA
ARKANSAS
Atlantic Ocean
MISSISSIPPI
ALABAMA
GEORGIA
TEXAS
FLORIDA
LOUISIANA
Gulf of Mexico
LEGEND
Home Stadium
Big Ten West
Big Ten East
United States
Other Countries
Water
SCALE
0 miles
500 miles
0 kilometers
500 km
N
E
S
W

The Uniforms

In 1939, the Riddell company invented the first plastic football helmet to increase player safety.

Coach Hayden Fry duplicated the Steelers' uniforms because he wanted his struggling players to identify with a successful team.

Hawkeye players wear the gold and black of the University of Iowa with pride. The colors have remained mostly unchanged over the years. The Hawkeyes' uniforms have had only small tweaks since the early days of Iowa football.

Today's uniforms feature gold pants with a black stripe. The home jersey is black with white numbers, while the away jersey is white with black numbers. The black helmet has the Hawkeye **logo** on both sides and a gold stripe running down the middle.

Fans of the National Football League (NFL) may notice similar-looking uniforms in Pittsburgh Steelers games. That is no coincidence. In 1979, Coach Hayden Fry asked the Steelers if he could have a uniform and a helmet to use as inspiration for the new Hawkeye uniforms. To this day, the Hawkeyes and the Steelers share a common look.

There have only been six times in the past 34 years that the Hawkeyes have worn helmet decals. One was a yellow sticker with the letters "ANF," which stood for "America Needs Farmers."

Student Athletes

During the 2017–18 season, **249** Iowa student athletes were selected to the **Academic All-Big Ten** team.

Iowa's defensive line, which includes Matt Hankins, Michael Ojemudia, and Geno Stone, helped the Hawkeyes defeat rivals the University of Nebraska Cornhuskers 31–28 in the final game of the 2018 regular season.

Being a college student athlete is hard work. Student athletes have to perform well on the football field and in the classroom. Iowa student athletes are required to meet a minimum grade point average and attend all of their classes. They must also have 12 academic credits per term. Iowa student athletes have access to the Russell and Ann Gerdin Athletic Learning Center, which provides students with tutoring, mentoring, and education about making healthy food choices. Athletes can even pick up a nutritious snack at the center.

Many student athletes are given athletic scholarships. An athletic scholarship is a financial aid agreement between the athlete and the college or university. Athletes who do not receive an athletic scholarship can be "walk-on" members of the team. This means they are on the team, but without athletic financial aid. Iowa typically awards the maximum number of football scholarships allowed, which is 85.

Running back Toren Young was the only sophomore appointed to the Hawkeyes' 2018 Leadership Group. The group is responsible for helping the coaches create team policies and make decisions for the good of the team.

Bowl Games

The **2009** Iowa team won the **Orange Bowl**, marking the first Bowl Championship Series win in school history.

Quarterback Nate Stanley's three touchdown passes led to the Hawkeyes' 27–22 win over Mississippi State University at the 2019 Outback Bowl.

Bowl games are a unique sports tradition in college football. In the beginning of college football, there was no true **postseason**. Today, a variety of postseason bowl games are played. Bowl games give teams the opportunity to continue striving for recognition and victory after the end of regular play. There are currently 40 bowl games played in various combinations each year. These games are chosen with input from teams, sponsors, and the College Football Playoff Selection Committee. The game matchups are announced in December.

The Hawkeyes have appeared in 32 bowl games over the years. They have a 16–15–1 record. Even more impressive is the fact that they have appeared in a bowl game every year since 2013. The team also won three bowl games in a row from 2008 to 2010, winning the Outback Bowl, the Orange Bowl, and the Insight Bowl.

The Hawkeyes fought until the end of the 2016 Rose Bowl, scoring two touchdowns in the fourth quarter, but the Stanford University Cardinal took the game, 45–16.

The Coaches

Kirk Ferentz has been with Iowa for **20 years**, the longest any current college football coach has been with a team.

Kirk Ferentz spent six seasons as an offensive line coach in the NFL before returning to Iowa as head coach in 1998.

The Iowa Hawkeyes have had 26 coaches since E. A. Dalton first led the team in 1892. They had 11 coaches in 34 years, but have only had 2 coaches since 1979, the least of any National Collegiate Athletic Association (NCAA) program. This head coaching stability has led to some of the greatest successes the team has seen.

HOWARD JONES Howard Jones is regarded by many as one of the greatest collegiate coaches of all time. He saw success with many schools, but his first extended job was with Iowa, where he led the Hawkeyes to a 42–17–1 record. Jones coached the Hawkeyes from 1916 to 1923 and led the team to two Big Ten championships.

HAYDEN FRY When Hayden Fry took over as head coach of the Hawkeyes, Iowa had not had a winning season in 17-straight years. That changed almost immediately with Fry in charge. From 1979 to 1998, he led the team to three Big Ten titles, 14 bowl appearances, and 143 wins. Fry was inducted into the College Football **Hall of Fame** in 2003.

KIRK FERENTZ The current coach of Iowa, Kirk Ferentz, was an assistant under Hayden Fry until 1989. When Fry retired in 1998, Ferentz was named head coach. Since then, the team has been to 16 bowl games, and Ferentz has been named Big Ten Coach of the Year four times. He has led the team to a 152–101 record and two Big Ten championships.

The Mascot

Since Herky is responsible for pumping up the crowd at games, he must be able to dance, jump, and run up and down the field. Herky also performs with the spirit squad and competes in the Mascot National Championship.

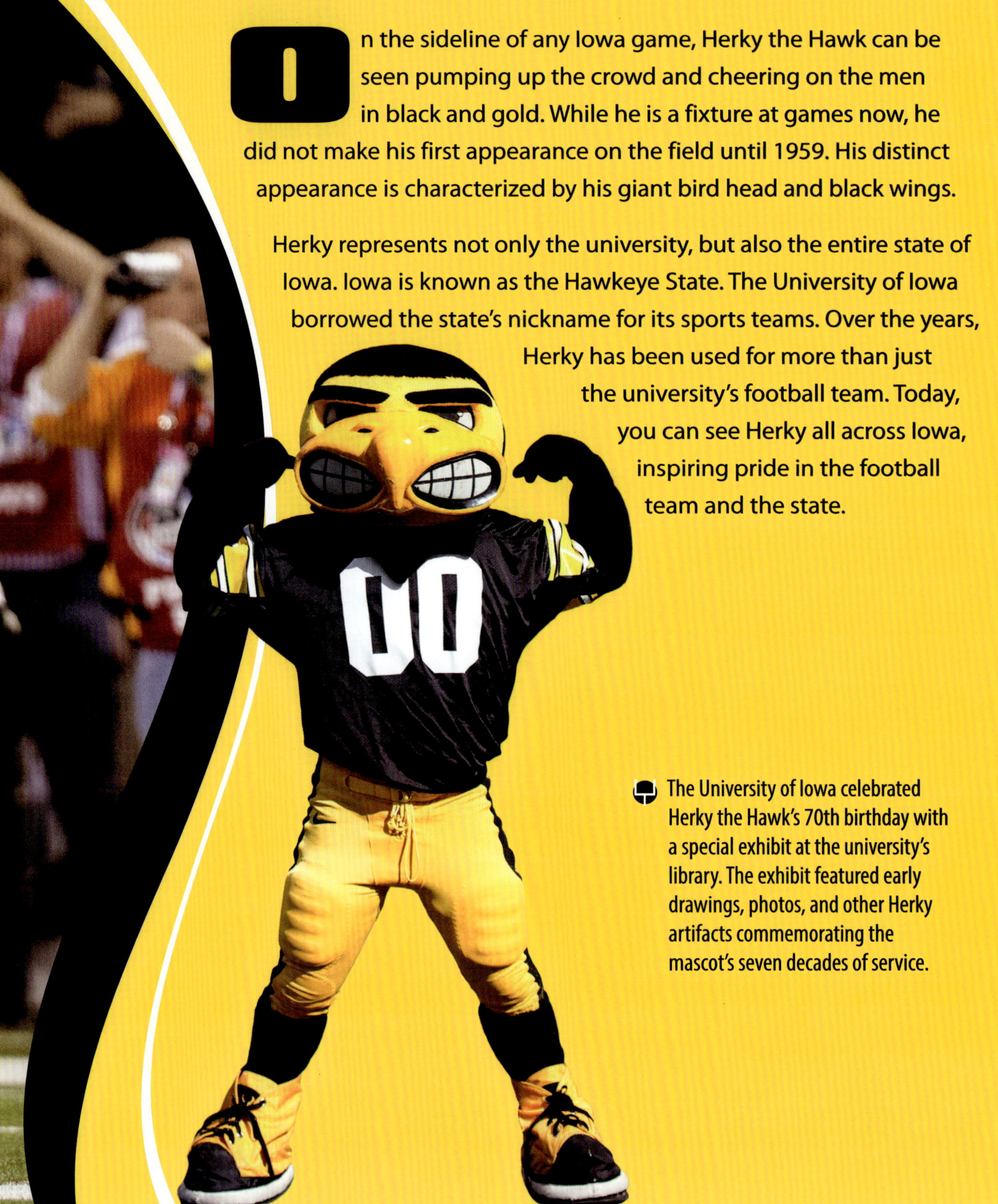

On the sideline of any Iowa game, Herky the Hawk can be seen pumping up the crowd and cheering on the men in black and gold. While he is a fixture at games now, he did not make his first appearance on the field until 1959. His distinct appearance is characterized by his giant bird head and black wings.

Herky represents not only the university, but also the entire state of Iowa. Iowa is known as the Hawkeye State. The University of Iowa borrowed the state's nickname for its sports teams. Over the years, Herky has been used for more than just the university's football team. Today, you can see Herky all across Iowa, inspiring pride in the football team and the state.

The University of Iowa celebrated Herky the Hawk's 70th birthday with a special exhibit at the university's library. The exhibit featured early drawings, photos, and other Herky artifacts commemorating the mascot's seven decades of service.

Legends of the Past

For many players, their time with the Hawkeyes is the start of a promising football career. These are some of the best-known football players to play for the University of Iowa.

Dallas Clark

Dallas Clark came to Iowa from Twin River Valley High School, where he was a standout linebacker. After not getting any playing time as a freshman and limited minutes as a sophomore, Clark moved to tight end before his junior year. That move turned out to be a good one. As a senior, Clark led the team to its first undefeated conference season in 80 years and won the John Mackey Award for most outstanding tight end in college football. Clark went on to be **drafted** 24th overall by the Indianapolis Colts in 2003. He retired in 2013.

Position: Tight End
Seasons: 1999–2002 (Iowa Hawkeyes), 2003–2011 (Indianapolis Colts), 2012 (Tampa Bay Buccaneers), 2013 (Baltimore Ravens)
Born: June 12, 1979, Sioux Falls, South Dakota

Andre Tippett

Pro Football Hall of Famer Andre Tippett got his start at the University of Iowa. In the 1980s, Tippett helped lead the Hawkeyes to their first Big Ten title in two decades. He was then drafted by the New England Patriots and was ultimately named to the NFL's All-Decade team for the 1980s. His most dominant stretch was from 1985 to 1987. For each of those three years, he was named linebacker of the year by the American Football Conference (AFC). He retired from the NFL in 1993. Tippett was inducted into the National Jewish Sports Hall of Fame in 2009.

Position: Linebacker
Seasons: 1979–1981 (Iowa Hawkeyes), 1982–1993 (New England Patriots)
Born: December 27, 1959, Birmingham, Alabama

Christian Kirksey

One of the most outstanding defensive players from Iowa in recent years, Christian Kirksey was named team captain his junior year. That season, he returned two interceptions for touchdowns. The next season, Kirksey helped lead the team to the Outback Bowl, and was named an All-Big Ten honorable mention. After Kirksey left Iowa, he was drafted in the third round by the Cleveland Browns. In 2016, he recorded a career-high 143 tackles. In 2017, the Browns re-signed Kirksey to a four-year, $38-million contract.

Position: Linebacker
Seasons: 2010–2013 (Iowa Hawkeyes), 2014–Present (Cleveland Browns)
Born: August 31, 1992, St. Louis, Missouri

Adrian Clayborn

Adrian Clayborn is one of the most feared defensive linemen in the NFL, but Iowa fans may know him best for the Orange Bowl **Most Valuable Player (MVP)** award he won in 2009. He finished that game with nine tackles and two **sacks**, helping to shut down the Georgia Tech Yellow Jackets' strong running game. In 2010, Clayborn was named a finalist for the Rotary Lombardi Award, which honors college football's best lineman or linebacker. Clayborn was drafted 20th overall in the 2011 draft by the Tampa Bay Buccaneers. He now plays for the New England Patriots.

Position: Defensive End
Seasons: 2006–2010 (Iowa Hawkeyes), 2011–2014 (Tampa Bay Buccaneers), 2015–2017 (Atlanta Falcons), 2018–Present (New England Patriots)
Born: July 6, 1988, St. Louis, Missouri

All-Time Records

484
Single-Season Points
The Hawkeyes scored 484 points in 2002, their most ever in a season.

70
Single-Game Points
The most points the Hawkeyes have scored in a game was 70 in 1957 against the Utah State University Aggies.

65
Career Completion Percentage
Chuck Long holds the school completion percentage record, completing 65 percent of his passes from 1981 to 1985.

4,156
Career Rushing Yards

Sedrick Shaw rushed for 4,156 yards in his career, an Iowa record.

9
Single-Game Sacks

The defense recorded nine sacks in a 1989 game against the Purdue University Boilermakers, the most it has ever scored in a single game.

Timeline

Throughout the team's history, the Iowa Hawkeyes have had many memorable events that have become defining moments for the team and its fans.

1889
The first Iowa Football team is formed.

1900

The Hawkeyes join the Western Conference, which later becomes the Big Ten, in 1899.

1919
Lester Belding is named Iowa's first consensus All-American.

1920

1939
Nile Kinnick wins the Heisman Trophy.

1940

1957
Iowa wins its first Rose Bowl.

1959
Herky the Hawk makes his first appearance.

1960

1961
The team finishes 5–4, its last winning season for 20 years.

1978
Hayden Fry takes over as head coach of the Hawkeyes.

1980

1999
Kirk Ferentz is hired to coach the team.

2000

2002
Brad Banks is elected the Associated Press College Football Player of the Year.

In 2005, the team has four Academic All-Americans, a school record.

2015
Iowa finishes the season ranked ninth in the nation.

2019
The team defeats the Mississippi State Bulldogs in the Outback Bowl in its second-straight bowl victory.

2020

The Future

Despite the tough competition in the Big Ten, the Hawkeyes are a force to be reckoned with year after year. They have not had a losing season since 2012. With the success of the current team, that does not look like it will be changing any time soon. The stability Coach Ferentz has created makes Iowa a place where plenty of football players find a way to play their very best.

Write a Biography

Life Story

A person's life story can be the subject of a book. This kind of book is called a biography. Biographies often describe the lives of people who have achieved great success. These people may be alive today, or they may have lived many years ago. Reading a biography can help you learn more about a great person.

Get the Facts

Use this book, and research in the library and on the internet, to find out more about your favorite player. Learn as much about him as you can. What position does he play? What are his statistics in important categories? Has he set any records? Also, be sure to write down key events in the person's life. What was his childhood like? What has he accomplished off the field? Is there anything else that makes this person special or unusual?

Use the Concept Web

A concept web is a useful research tool. Read the questions in the concept web on the following page. Answer the questions in your notebook. Your answers will help you write a biography.

Concept Web

Write a Biography

Adulthood
- Where does this individual currently reside?
- Does he have a family?

Your Opinion
- What did you learn from the books you read in your research?
- Would you suggest these books to others?
- Was anything missing from these books?

Childhood
- Where and when was this person born?
- Describe his parents, siblings, and friends.
- Did he grow up in unusual circumstances?

Accomplishments off the Field
- What is this person's life's work?
- Has he received awards or recognition for accomplishments?
- How have this person's accomplishments served others?

Help and Obstacles
- Did this individual have a positive attitude?
- Did he receive help from others?
- Did this person have a mentor?
- Did this person face any hardships?
- If so, how were the hardships overcome?

Accomplishments on the Field
- What records does this person hold?
- What key games and plays have defined his career?
- What are his stats in categories important to his position?

Work and Preparation
- What was this person's education?
- What was his work experience?
- How does this person work?
- What is the process he uses?

Trivia Time

Take this quiz to test your knowledge of the Iowa Hawkeyes.
The answers are printed upside down under each question.

1 When did the first Iowa football team play?

A. 1889

2 What conference is Iowa in?

A. The Big Ten

3 Who is the current coach of Iowa?

A. Kirk Ferentz

4 Which NFL team first drafted Dallas Clark?

A. The Indianapolis Colts

5 Which NFL team shares similar uniforms to the Hawkeyes?

A. The Pittsburgh Steelers

6 Which former Iowa player is in the Jewish Sports Hall of Fame?

A. Andre Tippett

7 What is the Iowa record for points scored in a single game?

A. 70

8 How many coaches have the Hawkeyes had since 1979?

A. Two

9 Which position did Christian Kirksey play?

A. Linebacker

10 Who was the first Hawkeye to win the Heisman Trophy?

A. Nile Kinnick

Key Words

drafted: chosen to play professionally in the National Football League during an annual event

Hall of Fame: a group of persons judged to be outstanding in a particular sport

Heisman Memorial Trophy: an annual award given to the college football player who best demonstrates excellence and hard work

logo: a symbol that stands for a team or organization

Most Valuable Player (MVP): the player judged to be most valuable to his team's success

postseason: a sporting event that takes place after the end of the regular season

renovations: construction that works to improve or expand an older building

sacks: when the quarterback, or another offensive player acting as a passer, is tackled behind the line of scrimmage before he can throw a forward pass

unity: being joined as a whole

unobstructed: free from obstacles

Index

Log on to www.av2books.com

AV² by Weigl brings you media enhanced books that support active learning. Go to www.av2books.com, and enter the special code found on page 2 of this book. You will gain access to enriched and enhanced content that supplements and complements this book. Content includes video, audio, weblinks, quizzes, a slideshow, and activities.

AV² Online Navigation

Book Pages
AV² pages directly correspond to pages in the book.

Key Words
Study vocabulary, and complete a matching word activity.

Quizzes
Test your knowledge.

Slideshow
View images and captions, and prepare a presentation.

Audio
Listen to sections of the book read aloud.

Video
Watch informative video clips.

Embedded Weblinks
Gain additional information for research.

Try This!
Complete activities and hands-on experiments.

AV² was built to bridge the gap between print and digital. We encourage you to tell us what you like and what you want to see in the future.

Sign up to be an AV² Ambassador at www.av2books.com/ambassador.

Due to the dynamic nature of the internet, some of the URLs and activities provided as part of AV² by Weigl may have changed or ceased to exist. AV² by Weigl accepts no responsibility for any such changes. All media enhanced books are regularly monitored to update addresses and sites in a timely manner. Contact AV² by Weigl at 1-866-649-3445 or av2books@weigl.com with any questions, comments, or feedback.